Tra dot

# Oedipus the King

BY SOPHOCLES

BrightSummaries.com

# SOPHOCLES

## GREEK PLAYWRIGHT

- **Born c. 496 B.C. in Athens**
- **Died c. 406 B.C. in the same city**
- **Notable works:**
  - *Antigone* (c. 442 B.C.), tragedy
  - *Philoctetes* (409 B.C.), tragedy
  - *Oedipus at Colonnus* (401 B.C., posthumous), tragedy

Sophocles is the best-known tragic poet in Ancient Greece, along with Aeschylus and Euripides. He was born c. 496 B.C. and died c. 406 B.C. He is the author of more than a hundred tragedies, only seven of which have come down to us, including *Oedipus the King* and *Antigone.* In Sophocles' plays, as opposed to those by his predecessor Aeschylus, the chorus (troop of people commenting the action through song or recitation) takes less place and the hero becomes psychologically deeper. Sophocles is often quoted as the leading figure of tragedy in Aristotle's *Poetics*.

# *OEDIPUS THE KING*

## *OEDIPUS THE KING*: A MODEL OF TRAGEDY

- **Genre:** play (tragedy)
- **Reference edition:** Sophocles (Unknown) *Oedipus the King*. [Online]. Trans. Grene, D. [Accessed 7 December 2015]. Available from: <http://abs.kafkas.edu.tr/upload/225/Oedipus_the_King_Full_Text.pdf>
- **First edition:** before 425 B.C.
- **Themes:** fate, transgression, incest, parricide, investigation, Thebes, mythology, Ancient Times

*Oedipus the King* is probably the archetype of tragedy, as this play stages a hero burdened with a destiny he cannot escape and he cannot accept. It is believed that the play was written some time before 425 B.C. It tells how Oedipus, King of Thebes, discovers that he has fulfilled the prophecy he was desperately trying to avoid and that, without knowing, he has murdered his father and married his mother. Learning the truth, Jocasta, his mother, commits suicide, while Oedipus gouges his own eyes out and asks to be sent into exile. Consequently, the play is a series of revelations, beginning with that of Teiresias, the blind yet clear-sighted seer.

# SUMMARY

In front of Oedipus' palace in Thebes, children are sitting on the steps and carrying olive branches. They are accompanied by a priest of Zeus. When Oedipus comes out to ask them about what is happening, the priest explains that Thebes is stricken by a plague:

> King, you yourself have seen our city reeling like a wreck already; it can scarcely lift its prow out of the depths, out of the bloody surf. A blight is on the fruitful plants of the earth. A blight is on the cattle in the fields, a blight is on our women that no children are born to them; a God that carries fire, a deadly pestilence, is on our town, strikes us and spears us not, and the house of Cadmus is emptied of its people while black Death grows rich in groaning and in lamentation (lines 13-33).

He asks for Oedipus' help.

Creon, Jocasta's brother, who had gone to fetch the word of the gods, comes back and tells them that the death of Laius, the king who governed the city before Oedipus, must be avenged, in order for the plague to recede. However, nobody knows who killed that king. Oedipus decides to conduct an investigation: "I will bring this to light again" (line 161). He goes back into the palace with Creon. The children leave, while a chorus of old men complaining about the tragic situation of the city arrives: Oedipus answers them: "For what you ask me – if you will hear my words" (line 232). He proceeds to enlist their help in order to shed light on the matter.

Oedipus retells how he came to succeed Laius and marry his wife, Jocasta. As he owes so much to this man who he never met, he says: "Because of all these things, I fight in his defense as for my father" (lines 283-284). The chorus leader suggests that Oedipus interrogate Teiresias, who has the gift of clear-sightedness. Teiresias enters, led by a child. Oedipus asks him what he knows and the seer answers: "Alas, how terrible is wisdom when it brings no profit to the man that's wise!" (Lines 347-348), and refuses to tell more. Oedipus insists and Teiresias finally tells the truth: "I say you are the murderer of the king whose murderer you seek" (line 415-416). He adds: "I say with those you love best you live in foulest shame unconsciously and do not see where you are in calamity" (lines 422-423).

Oedipus believes that Creon, jealous of his power, has schemed to have these words uttered to compromise him. Teiresias leaves and Oedipus goes into the palace. Creon, who has heard it said that Oedipus accuses him, wants to confront him to know the truth: "If he believes that in these present troubles he has been wronged by me in word or deed I do not want to live on with the burden of such a scandal on me" (lines 595-598). Oedipus then arrives who interrogates him about Teiresias and the murder of Laius. Jocasta protests. Oedipus continues to believe Creon to be guilty. However, convinced by the chorus, he agrees to ask for Creon's exile rather than his death.

Jocasta tells Oedipus that seers are sometimes mistaken, as Laius had been told that he would be killed by his son, while he was assassinated by common thieves. Hearing this,

Oedipus starts to understand that he might have killed his own father. He tells his story: as one day, someone called him a bastard, he started having doubts as to the identity of his true parents and fled; on the way he killed an unknown man.

A messenger from Corinth arrives to announce the death of Polybus, the man Oedipus believed to be his father. However, he also adds that Polybus was not Oedipus' true father, that he himself had found him as a child and had given him to Polybus. A herdsman of King Laius had given the infant to the messenger. Jocasta reacts violently upon hearing this: "O Oedipus, God help you! God keep you from the knowledge of who you are!" (lines 1222-1223) and then she goes back into the palace. Oedipus interrogates the herdsman and finally learns that it was Jocasta who had given him the child for him to kill it, but that, overwhelmed by pity, he had spared it. Before running to the palace, he exclaims: "O, O, O, they will all come, all come out clearly! Light of the sun, let me look upon you no more after today! I who first saw the light bred of a match accursed and accursed in my living with them I lived with, cursed in my killing" (lines 1363-1368).

Then the messenger announces the death of Jocasta, who has hung herself, and proceeds to explain that Oedipus, taking the golden brooches from his mother's clothing, gouged out his eyes. Oedipus, now blind, appears. He asks Creon to exile him and to take good care of his daughters. The leader of the chorus concludes with these words: "Count no mortal happy till he has passed the final limit of his life secure from pain" (lines 1729-1732).

# CHARACTER STUDY

## OEDIPUS

Oedipus is King of Thebes. He is married to Jocasta and they have several children. He is a foreigner to the city because he has been raised by Polybus of Corinth and Merope, a Dorian, whom he believes to be his real parents. In truth, he is the son of Laius, the former King of Thebes, and of Jocasta. At birth, Jocasta had given him to a herdsman to be killed, but, seized by pity, the herdsman had spared him and gave him to another man who in turn gave him to King Polybus. Oedipus must therefore discover his true identity. His whole life has been an illusion and in the play, the dark tragedy of his existence is slowly brought to life: he has killed his father and married his mother.

At the beginning of the play, Oedipus is loved and admired. He is the one who saved Thebes, the one who solved the riddle of the sphinx, and the one to whom the priest turns spontaneously when misery seizes the city once again. The priest tells him:

> We have not come as suppliants to this altar because we thought of you as a God, but rather judging you the first of men in all the chances of this life and when we mortals have to do with more that man. You came and by your coming saved our city, freed us from the tribute which we paid of old to the Sphinx, cruel singer. This you did in virtue of no knowledge we could give you, in virtue of no teaching; it was God that aided you, men say, and you are held with God's assistance to have saved our lives. (lines 34-45)

Oedipus seems to be fearless and thirsty for knowledge. He decides to conduct an enquiry into the murder of Laius and often plays the role of the interrogator in the play. However, he is also fiery and often succumbs to his passion. For example, when he starts doubting Creon, no argument manages to change his mind. Later, when he begins to glimpse the truth, Jocasta says of him that: "For Oedipus excites himself too much at every sort of trouble, not conjecturing, like a man of sense, what will be from what was" (1037-1039).

Out of despair for his fate, he gouges his eyes out. He ends up being the victim of the curse he inflicted himself on the author of the crime, namely exile. As highlighted by Teiresias: "Misery shall grind no man as it will you" (line 501). Oedipus is the character who climbed the highest and who, in a tragic reversal of fortune, has fallen down and lost everything.

## JOCASTA AND CREON

They are both opposites of Oedipus, as interlocutors, as well as doubles. Jocasta is the second tragic character of the play. She follows the same path as Oedipus, from present to past, from falsehood to truth. Upon discovering her unconscious crime of incest, she commits suicide by hanging.

However, throughout the whole play, she was the one who stayed optimistic and reassuring. She stood between Oedipus and Creon to calm their disagreement; she tried to convince Oedipus that the seer was mistaken. Nonetheless, all she does is deliberately blinding herself, as does Oedipus. Her character balances between a maternal figure and that of a woman who asked for her son to be murdered and finally married him unknowingly.

Creon, in comparison, is the loyal and reasonable character of the play. To Oedipus' bursts of anger, he opposes a well-argued and solid speech. When Oedipus wants to sentence him to death, he answers:

> Go to the oracle at Pytho and inquire about the answers, if they are as I told you. For the rest, if you discover that I laid any plot together with the seer, kill me, I say, not only by your vote but by my own. But do not charge me on obscure opinion without some proof to back it. It's not just lightly to count your knaves as honest men, nor with honest men as knaves. To throw away an honest friend is, as it were, to throw your life away, which a man loves the best. (lines 703-714)

Moreover, he is the one Oedipus trusts at the end of the play, asking him to take care of his daughters during his exile.

## THE CHORUS, TEIRESIAS AND THE OTHER CHARACTERS

Led by the chorus leader, and located below the orchestra, the chorus, in Greek tragedy, interacts with the actors who play the characters and are on stage. Over the course of time, the role of the chorus decreased in Greek theater, but in Sophocles' works, it is still important and takes part in the action, as opposed to the later plays by Euripides (Greek tragedy playwright, 484-406 B.C.). The parts of the text assigned to the chorus are sung. In *Oedipus the King*, the chorus is made up of old men who represent the voice of the city. They comment on the action and the revelations, and often highlight the pathos of the scenes that have just happened: "In the unnumbered death of its people the city dies; those children that are born lie dead on the naked earth unpitied, spreading contagion of death" (lines 203-207).

The other characters play mainly an informative role. They intervene at moments in the action to disclose what they know. This is the case with the servant, the herdsman and the messenger. Among them, Teiresias plays a more important role. He is a seer, and therefore, like the oracle, he is an intermediary between gods and mortals. He knows things that the rest of mankind ignores. Oedipus tells him when he welcomes him "Teiresias, you are versed in everything, things teachable and things not to be spoken, things of the heaven and earth-creeping things. You have no eyes but in your mind you know with what a plague our city is afflicted" (lines 326-330). Symbolically, he represents the exact opposite of Oedipus: he is blind, but he sees the truth, while Oedipus sees, but lives in an illusion. When Oedipus discovers the truth, he blinds himself physically, unable to bear the truth he is offered. The knowledge of the truth is a burden. This is what Teiresias has already said at the beginning of the play: "All of you here know nothing. I will not bring to light of day my troubles, mine—rather than call them yours" (lines 365-367).

# ANALYSIS

## AN INVESTIGATION

The play is constructed around a double investigation: the real investigation into the murder of Laius, and the hidden investigation of Oedipus' identity. At the beginning, not only does the king not know where to start, but he is also told lies. He says: "Where would a trace of this old crime be found?" (lines 127-128). It is believed that Laius has been killed by thieves, although it is a lie. Polybus and Merope also had Oedipus believe that he was truly their son, which is also a lie. The goal is to replace the fictitious accounts with the truth.

A big part of the play consists of an exchange of questions and answers, of dialogues that turn into interrogations. Oedipus says: "What I say to you, I say as one that is a stranger to the story as stranger to the deed. For I would not be far upon the track if I alone were tracing it without a clue" (lines 234-238). Witnesses are heard, among whom the herdsman, and experts are called, such as Teiresias. They each defend their perspective when the time of accusation arrives. Oedipus, when he is accused by Teiresias, as he doesn't have any arguments to defend himself, retaliates by denouncing a conspiracy against him.

Because of these investigations, there is little action in the play. It involves a return to the past, as that is what made the present what it is. Nothing happens but the discovery of the past. The only actions, namely Jocasta's suicide and

Oedipus' mutilation, which take place away from the stage, are only the consequences of the disclosure of that past. These actions are a form of tragic acceptance of the past.

## ORDER AND TRANSGRESSION

The investigation is born from a desire to restore an order which had been unsettled. The oracle, word from the gods, requests that the murder of the previous king be avenged. The plague striking Thebes represents this change in the order of things. The murder of the king is a fundamental transgression in itself, but for Oedipus this crime is also a parricide.

Oedipus is the character of the ultimate transgression, as he is guilty both of parricide and incest. These two prohibitions are the very foundations of a society. Teiresias tells Oedipus: "With those you love best you live in foulest shame unconsciously and do not see where you are in calamity" (lines 422-424). Oedipus unconsciously broke the order of things. However, he was the man who restored order by freeing Thebes from the sphinx. Oedipus is the hero, the character whose actions are precisely on the side of order and transgression and whose destiny has an impact on the whole of society.

## A TRAGIC ITINERARY

The main characteristic in *Oedipus the King* is the emphasis that lies with the tragic irony. The gods do not appear in the play, but their words are passed on through the oracle. The oracles are mysterious and do not enable the characters to escape their fates. On the contrary, they contribute to provoking it. Oedipus says: "But Phoebus sent me home again unhonored in what I came to learn, but he foretold other and desperate horrors to befall me, that I was fated to lie with my mother, and show to daylight an accursed breed which men would not endure, and I was doomed to be murderer of the father that begot me" (lines 919-925). Thus, the oracle did not answer Oedipus' question on his identity, but simply gives him information that he cannot understand and which therefore cannot help him to overcome his destiny. For fearing of making this prophecy come true, he goes to Thebes, far from Polybus and Merope, but it is by going to Thebes that he fulfills his destiny without knowing it, as he kills his father on the way and marries his mother. This is the very principle of tragic irony: the character believes to be acting in his interest, while in fact his heading for his downfall.

Aristotle (Greek philosopher, 384-322 B.C.), in his *Poetics*, explains that the function of tragedy is to trigger a catharsis in the spectator, i.e. a cleaning of passions. The action on stage causes the audience to feel fear then pity, therefore liberating their feelings, in a way. *Oedipus the King* is in perfect symbiosis with this model of tragedy, as the terrible story of Oedipus awakens these two feelings simultaneously in all the characters of the play, in the chorus, and consequently, in the audience itself.

The element of tragedy implies a specific relation to time, which is already distinct in the play: in the tragic universe, everything has already happened. Everything is planned in advance, as shown by the oracles, but more importantly, the core action happened in the past. No other action is possible, except for telling what happened and discovering the truth.

# FURTHER REFLECTION

## SOME QUESTIONS TO THINK ABOUT...

- Follow the evolution of the characters of Jocasta and Oedipus throughout the play.
- Analyze Creon's behavior and his dialogues with Oedipus. What is his role?
- What is the role of the chorus? In your opinion, is it important?
- How are the interventions of the chorus defined? What tone do they use?
- Which and in what order are the revelations that progressively lead to the full disclosure of the past events?
- How is Oedipus a tragic hero?
- No action actually takes place on stage. Everything happened already before the story began. Justify this statement.
- The history of Oedipus' family is a succession of transgressions and crimes. What happens to the other members of the family?
- Freud, the famous psychologist of the early 20$^{th}$ century, analyzed what he called the Oedipus complex. What is this? Explain this concept.

*We want to hear from you!*
*Leave a comment on your online library*
*and share your favourite books on social media!*

# FURTHER READING

## REFERENCE EDITION


- Sophocles (Unknown) *Oedipus the King*. [Online]. Trans. Grene, D. [Accessed 7 December 2015]. Available from: <http://abs.kafkas.edu.tr/upload/225/Oedipus_the_King_Full_Text.pdf>

www.brightsummaries.com

Ebook EAN: 9782806273444

Paperback EAN: 9782806273451

Legal Deposit: D/2015/12603/596

Cover: © Primento

Digital conception by Primento, the digital partner of publishers.

16249294R10016

Printed in Poland
by Amazon Fulfillment
Poland Sp. z o.o., Wrocław